The Kids' Allowance Book

The Kids' Allowance Book

Amy Nathan
Illustrations by Debbie Palen

AN AUTHORS GUILD BACKINPRINT.COM EDITION

AN AUTHORS GUILD BACKINPRINT.COM EDITION

Published by iUniverse, Inc.

For information address:
iUniverse, Inc.
2021 Pine Lake Road, Suite 100
Lincoln, NE 68512
www.iuniverse.com

Originally published by Walker and Company

Book design by Dede Cummings and John Reinhardt

ISBN-13: 978-0-595-39106-6
ISBN-10: 0-595-39106-0

Printed in the United States of America

For
Noah, Eric, and Carl

Contents

The Kids' Allowance Book

Lots of Questions

For answers to questions about *invisible, shrinking, disappearing, never-on-time, fizzled, flopped,* and even *dishpan-hands* allowances, ask the experts: kids! This book has a whole squad of experts—an Allowance All-Star Squad of 166 kids.

These nine- to fourteen-year-olds all get an allowance—a special sum of money they receive regularly from their parents—and come from eleven schools across the country, from Maine to California. To land a spot on the All-Star roster, they had to sweat their way through a tough workout—filling out a four-page questionnaire that asked all about their allowance and what they did with it. This book presents a picture of how these kids' allowances really work.

Kids on the All-Star Squad set up their allowances in different ways; there's no "right way" to do it. They've also come up with clever strategies for handling some of the common allowance gripes. So have their parents, several of whom share their views on allowances in this book and even reveal what works best in talking parents into giving kids a raise!

Besides tips from Allowance All Stars and their parents, this book pulls together information on allowances from other sources. You may pick up some ideas that can whip your allowance into better shape. Or if you're new to the allowance game, this book can help you decide whether an allowance is for you and how to get it going.

Is an Allowance a Good Deal?

WHAT'S THE SCORE? IS AN ALLOWANCE REALLY WORTH GETTING?

What a Hit!

Allowances score high with our Allowance All-Star Squad (the 166 kids around the country who gave us the lowdown on their money). Almost all like getting an allowance—that oh-so-welcome chunk of money their parents hand out once a week (or in some cases every two weeks, or once a month). Here's why an allowance wins so many fans.

■ **Cool cash.** "It's money! Who doesn't want it?" says Lauren. The cash definitely appeals to her Squad mates, too.

■ **A sure thing.** But it's not just the cash; it's that it comes in so *regularly*. You can count on getting it, without going through a big hassle each time. "If I didn't get an allowance, I'd

have to ask my parents for money to get *everything* I want," says Charles. "An allowance makes me feel like I don't have to depend on my parents for everything," notes Amanda B. Julia adds: "It makes me feel more grown-up."

■ **Hot stuff.** Matt notes another allowance advantage: "I can buy things I want." (As long as they're not on your parents' totally off-limits list, of course.) "Before I got an allowance, my parents didn't always buy me what I wanted," Katie explains. "If I wanted a pair of special sneakers, they might say it's too expensive and not a necessity. Now that I get an allowance, if they don't want to pay, I can pay for it myself."

■ **Super stash.** Some of our All Stars have been getting an allowance only for about a year. They remember how tough it was to save when they got money just every now and then, not regularly. An allowance makes saving easier. "You know how much money you'll have each week," says Desirée. You can set a goal and

WHO?

WISE BUYER

know when you'll reach it. If you want an expensive game, you can tell *exactly* when you can buy it if you set aside half your allowance a week for it. Of course, many no-allowance kids are super savers, too, but some surveys have found that allowance kids tend to do a bit better at this.

■ **Money wise.** "My allowance helps me realize I need to be careful and not blow my money," says Jamie. Rashaun's allowance shows him "you can't just go out and buy something. You have to wait until you'll have some cash left over for the next thing." Katie has learned to s-t-r-e-t-c-h her allowance by looking for low prices. "I'm more careful with *my* money than with my parents' money,"

she admits. "If I waste my allowance on something I don't need, I won't have any for something I really want."

She and other Squad members goofed up a bit at first with their allowance. But, hey, isn't it better to learn with small sums than to goof up big time with big bucks later? Most kids on our Squad say hav-

HMMMM...

... AND IF I GET AN ALLOWANCE, I WON'T HAVE TO ASK YOU FOR MONEY ALL THE TIME!

> **QUICK CHANGE**
>
> Most teens with allow-ances save part of their allowance each week.
>
> SOURCE: Liberty Financial Young Investor Survey, 1993.

ing an allowance to mess around with gives them a great chance to learn how to become money smart.

It also gives them time to practice another skill: negotiating with parents. Planning an allowance (and keeping it running) takes a lot of talking and bargaining with parents. "That will pay off down the line in all the conversations on *other* issues that come up between parents and kids," says Dr. Jonathan Bloomberg, a psychiatrist and allowance-giving dad. By talking with parents about your allowance, "you can show that your opinion counts and that you and your parents can solve conflicts together." That can help you feel ready to tackle other, tougher problems together later on.

Who Gets It-Who Doesn't

About half of nine- to fourteen-year-olds get an allowance, according to surveys done by such groups as *Zillions* magazine and Nickelodeon TV. The number getting allowances tends to go down as kids move into their late teens, probably because many older teens have part-time jobs. At what age do allowances start? Most members of our Allowance Squad were seven to eleven when they first got one. But a few began as early as age five—or as late as age thirteen.

Kids who *don't* get allowances—about 110 of them—also filled out questionnaires for this book. Do they get spending money? Sure—in handouts from parents, as birthday or holiday gifts, or as pay for doing chores at home or jobs for others. Many of them *used* to get an allowance. Some feel they do better without one since their parents usually hand out cash when asked. "If I got an allowance, there'd be a limit to what I could get," a girl says. Others earn a lot from jobs like baby-sitting and don't need an allowance. But most wish they got one. Either they don't always get money if they ask, or jobs are hard to find. As one boy says, he's ready for more "steady pay."

On Your Mark, Get Set . . .

If you don't get an allowance but want to, how do you talk parents into starting one? Here's what our All Stars did.

■ **Smart-money strategy.** "I said I wouldn't waste my money if they gave me an allowance," notes Lauren. Smart move, especially if you explain how you'll keep your spending under control. After all, money management is a main goal parents have for allowances, according to parents of Squad members. These parents note another parent-pleasing plus: Maybe managing an allowance can even help boost math skills.

• A CLOSER LOOK •

Lauren's Better Gifts

"Before I got an allowance, I didn't have much money and couldn't buy birthday presents for my friends," says Lauren. "If I was going to a birthday party, my parents bought the present." Now, Lauren saves up her allowance—and buys better gifts. "My parents might have wanted to spend only $5 on the gift, but if I see something nicer for more, I can buy it if I have the money. I like giving my friends better presents."

■ **Friends factor.** Lauren also told her mom that "some of my friends

> *"I can buy things
> I want."*

got an allowance. But I was careful how I said it. I didn't go, '*Everyone* gets one but me!'" Parents *hate* that. She casually dropped a few friends' names. That got her mom to talk with the mom of one of those friends to learn more about allowances.

■ **Nuisance control.** Katie told her parents that getting an allowance would end her "always having to ask them for money." To help make this point, keep a list for a few weeks of how many, *many* times you bug your parents for cash. Point out that not only is an allowance less of a nuisance, it doesn't have to increase parents' costs. "You're simply shifting them. An allowance is a way of sharing family income and shifting some age-appropriate expenses to children," says Elissa Buie, a financial planner and allowance-giving mom. Pick the purchases you feel ready to take over, like snacks or hobby supplies. Talk with your parents about how much they usually spend on you for that. Ask if that part of the family budget can be turned over to you to handle—as an allowance.

■ **Pop a plan.** "Before I got an allowance, I thought of a way to keep track of my work and how much my parents would owe me," says Larry. "I set up a chart and showed it to my mom." Was she impressed? You bet! They still had lots to talk about before she decided to start the allowance, but his chart got things rolling. Larry offered to do chores for his allowance, but there are other ways to go. To pick a plan to pop on your parents, read on.

The Great Chores Debate

A Sweaty Tale

Sorry about those dishpan hands, pal, but most kids on our Allowance Squad have to sweat their way to allowance payday, doing chores. Several research studies have found the same thing—that most kids have to do chores for their allowance.

How many chores do our Squad mates have to do? A few do one; others slog through six a week or more! The average is three chores a week. Some chores have to be done just once a week. Others have to be tackled every day. Leading the list is cleaning their rooms—half the kids have to do that for their allowance. Other biggies: dishwashing, vacuuming, floor sweeping, bathroom cleaning, lawn mowing, table setting, pet care, as well as garbage or laundry duty. Kids also do other things, depending on their families' needs. For example, a few kids earn allowance by baby-sitting a younger brother or sister.

But one out of four Squad members has a different kind of allowance—one not tied to chores at all. They get paid even if they sometimes forget to make their beds or change the kitty litter.

Kids and parents have strong feelings about whether to link an allowance to chores. This debate has been going on for about 100 years, ever since many American families first started giving kids an allowance. Read on to catch both sides of the debate.

> ### QUICK CHANGE
> A poll of 2,000 *Money* magazine readers (grown-ups, most likely) found that about one out of three thought an allowance should NOT be linked to chores—but two out of three thought it should.
>
> SOURCE: *Money*,
> October 1993, p. 31.

Why Link It to Chores?

"I like doing chores for my allowance," says Amanda B. "You learn you have to work for things instead of people just giving you things all the time. It's preparing me for later when I'll get a real job." Giving kids a chance to learn firsthand about the connection between work and money is one big reason many kids and parents choose a chores allowance. As Matt's mom says, she wants Matt to "earn his money like in the real world."

Some parents also have other reasons. "Our goal is to give Derek a sense of accomplishment," his mom reports. "To teach him responsibility not only for money but for getting a job done and doing it well enough to get some recognition." Larry's mom wants her son to realize that by being paid for chores "he plays an important role in the family." Plus she hopes he'll begin to appreciate "what it's like to keep the household going."

...AND I BELIEVE THAT *CHORES* ARE WHAT KEEP OUR CHILDREN STRONG!

PARENT

KID

THE GREAT CHORES DEBATE

Stephen's mom has a few more practical goals in mind, such as "getting help with the housework and encouraging him to pick up after himself and keep his room neater." Is the plan working? Yep! "He takes more pride in how his room looks," she says.

Why Not?

Now for the other side of the debate. Jennifer doesn't *have* to finish a certain number of chores to collect her allowance. "If I help out, it should be because I want to," she explains. "Because everybody has to pitch in." She is usually pretty good about pitching in, doing her best to tidy up and keep her room clean.

It's easy to see why an allowance that's *not* tied to chores might be a hit with kids like Jennifer. But it's also popular with psychologists, who worry that a chores-based allowance may give you the wrong idea—that you'll get paid for *every* little thing you do.

Amanda's Freebies

Our Allowance All Stars don't get paid for every little thing they do at home. They do plenty of freebies. On top of all the cleaning and garbage toting Amanda B. has to do for her allowance, she regularly does freebies like folding the clothes or setting the table. "If I'm sitting around and my mom asks me to do something, I'll say sure and won't ask to get paid," she says. "I do it to help out."

But if she is saving up for something special, she'll hunt for a big job that needs doing, such as basement cleaning. *Ugh!* She'll ask if her mom will pay extra for it. That's when the freebies pay off. "Since I'm not always working just for money, when I ask if she'll pay me to do something extra, she usually does."

"That's not necessarily the way it works," warns one psychologist, Dr. Ken Doyle. "There are things that should be done just because they're the right things to do, even things that aren't fun (like taking out the garbage). Someone has to do it. It's not fair to con Mom into doing it all the time." Also, what if you're rolling in dough and don't need allowance one week? "You can't abandon your responsibility to wash the dishes or walk the dog just because you have enough cash one week," says another psychologist, Dr. Lawrence Kutner. "We all have to pitch in because we're members of a family, not because we need spending money."

Emily and her family note another reason why they don't link her allowance to chores: Emily's allowance got started to help her learn to be money wise. If the allowance was tied to chores and she skipped a chore and the allowance got cut, she'd lose out on the money she was supposed to learn how to manage.

Time Out

What about a compromise? That's how several Allowance All Stars and their families solved the Great Chores Debate. They found ways to combine *both* types of allowance. For example, there can be a basic allowance that's *not* tied to chores at all, that kids get no matter what. Then, kids can sometimes earn *more* by doing special "extra" chores at home. That's the kind of setup Jennifer and her family use.

"You learn you have to work for things instead of people just giving you things all the time."

"It's like a sports contract. There's a base salary, and the extra chores are like incentive clauses," says Dr. Bloomberg, a psychiatrist who uses this approach with his family, too. He likes it because "if a child has a bad week, there's still money coming in. The base salary can be low, with the bonus clauses higher. So if you work harder, it pays off—an important lesson."

You Make the Call

"There's no one right way," says Dr. Kutner. Although he prefers not linking an allowance to chores, he notes "this is not necessarily for everyone." Most kids on our Allowance Squad are happy with their allowance, whether it's tied to chores or not. They have found that either approach can work if it's set up carefully and if kids and parents really try to make a go of it.

Do kids who have a chores allowance turn into money maniacs who won't lift a finger around the house unless they're paid? Nope. Many pitch in for free, doing chores that aren't part of their allowance. What about kids who don't have a chores allowance—are they lazy bums? Of course not! They get their hands dirty (or dusty or sudsy) doing housework, too. As Emily says, "With the allowance money coming in, I feel guilty about why other people should do all the work. So I help out."

Which would work best for you—an allowance linked to chores or not? That's something to chat about with your parents. But turning thumbs-up or -down on chores is just the first step. Read on for other choices to make in designing an allowance plan.

"If I help out, it should be because I want to. Because everybody has to pitch in."

Allowance Plans

Pick and Choose

To build an allowance plan, you need a little imagination and a bit of time. Time for you and your parents to talk over your goals for the allowance. Time to sort through the oodles of ways there are to set up an allowance. Time to cook up your own personal plan.

This chapter describes the basic plans and options used by kids on our Allowance Squad. Of

AL-LOW-ANCE! MUST HAVE ONE! BUT HOW TO BUILD IT? WITH LASER BEAMS? OR INTERGALACTIC GLUE? OR...

course, there are always other ways to do things, but the ideas that follow should get you started in thinking about what might work for you. Maybe you'll dream up a brand-new plan all your own!

As you put together your allowance plan, keep in mind that it needs to be one you can *really* carry out—week in and week out. Don't make it so complicated that it might crash in a few weeks.

Even if your allowance is already rolling along, the choices that follow may give you some fresh ideas to perk up your plan.

Chores Plan

Most kids on our Allowance Squad use a Chores Plan—they have to do chores to get their allowance. But not every Chores Plan works the same.

■ **Who chooses.** In some families, parents select the chores. In other families, parents and kids choose together. "We both think of things that need to be done and that I am capable of doing," reports Michael. Amanda's mom started things off by making a list of chores.

"Then I picked chores I wouldn't mind doing, like cleaning bathrooms," says Amanda B. (No kidding, she actually *likes* this job.) "That way it's not so bad," she says. "But if your mom chooses, she might give you a chore you can't even bear the *thought* of doing." If you skip that hated chore, your parents may skip paying you. Whoever does the picking should make sure the jobs are ones you can (and *will*) do.

■ **How many.** The number of chores differ. The average? Three per week. (See page 12 for more on the chores kids do.)

■ **Same or different.** Trent does the same chores each week for his allowance: cleans his room, washes dishes, sweeps the floor. Not Katie. "It gets boring," she says. Usually she has dishwasher duty, but some weeks she may vacuum instead. "My chores list changes every week," she explains. "Each week my parents give me choices on what I can do."

■ **Checks and charts.** Many kids use a chart to keep track of chores. "Dad makes a new chart each week to put on the refrigerator," Derek says. "The chart has columns and lines. The days of the week are along the top. A chore is listed on each line down the side. After I do a chore, I check off the space for that chore. At the end of the week I show the chart to my parents to get paid. I like it because it shows how responsible you were." It can also settle disputes about whether you really did a job (if you're good about always jotting down those check marks).

Kelly's chart is more like a poster. It lists all the chores each kid in

MY CHORES	SUN.	MON.	TUES.	WED.	THUR.	FRI.	SAT.
CLEAN ROOM	✓		✓	✓			✓
SWEEP KITCHEN FLOOR	✓	✓			✓		✓
FEED SPIKE	✓	✓	✓	✓	✓	✓	✓
CHANGE IGGY'S CAGE		✓			✓		

DOG SHOW

ADMIT ONE

the family has to do. "Mom wrote it and put it on the back door. It's updated yearly," says Kelly. "It's a good way to keep things fair so we know we all have to do our share."

■ **Penalty box.** "If I don't do the chores, I don't get paid," notes Derek. Most Chores Plan kids lose money for slacking off. Some won't get any allowance that week. Others get

• A CLOSER LOOK •

Charles's Lucky Break

Charles has found a way to stop singing the ol' dishpan-hands blues (at least, to stop singing them *every* day). "I rotate doing dishes with my brother and sister," he says. "One week I do the dishes; one week they do them. So we get a break before having to do them again."

Dish patrol is just one of the chores they have to do for their allowance. Each kid also has another chore that doesn't rotate—one that each of them has to do every day. Charles's daily chore is taking care of his dog. "I volunteered to do that," he says. "I like it."

only part of it (some cash gets knocked off for each chore not done). But Derek's mom says she won't cut the allowance if there are special reasons for skipping a chore (such as the kid is sick or has an unbelievable amount of homework). To figure how much to subtract, some parents glance at the check-off chart to see which jobs weren't done. Another method: At the start of a week, the total amount of the allowance *in coins* goes in a jar. Each time a chore is skipped, a parent takes out a coin. At week's end, the kid gets what is left in the jar.

OH I GOT THOSE WASHIN' BLUES!

But not everyone loses cash for undone chores. "I still get my allowance if I don't do all my chores, but I have to make up the chores," says Katie. So do about one-third of the Chores Plan kids. Either they have to do the skipped chore or an extra one instead. A few unlucky kids suffer a different fate when they forget a chore—they get grounded.

■ **Bonus prize.** Stephen's mom has found a way to make him really want to do *all* his chores. "As he does a chore, he checks it off on a chart. At the end of the week, if all chores were done, he earns his allowance *plus* a star," says his mom. "Stars can be saved up for a lunch out or a toy or game."

Choose-It Plan

With a Choose-It Plan, instead of having a set number of chores to do, kids decide for themselves each week from a long list of possibilities how many they will do. "Mom and I came up with a list of thirty chores that I have on a chart—a plain piece of paper I put on my wall," says Manda. "I get to choose which chores to do each week. When I do one, I put a check next to it on my chart. If I make my bed every day, that's seven checks. If I get fifty checks in a week, I get my allowance. If I don't get fifty checks, I have to start over the next week."

Other kids have a list of chores with a *price* next to each. After doing a chore, they put a check by it. At week's end, a parent adds up the checks and prices to figure how much allowance to pay that week.

Not many kids on our team use a Choose-It Plan. It probably works best with go-getters who don't mind housework. It would be a disaster for chores haters who might never check off anything, no matter how long the list of choices.

Just-Because Plan

Kids on this plan don't have to do chores to get allowance money. They get it "just because" they are members of the family. "I want to encourage helping out around the house just because it's needed, not because of how much you'll get paid," says one mom. With this plan, there's no checking up to see who did what, so there's less chance for things to go wrong. About one out of four kids on our Allowance Squad has a Just-Because allowance. Do they ever do chores? "Yes," says Jennifer, who is expected to keep her room clean and make her bed. "But that's not how I get my allowance."

■ **Getting tough.** What if chores *don't* get done? What can parents do if they can't threaten to hold back the allowance? "They just tell me to do it and I do it," says Kyle, who usually sets the table and helps make dinner. Emily's mom notes: "We *expect* Emily to do chores. She doesn't have the choice *not* to do them, so tying them to an allowance wouldn't make sense." Bridget's parents use a different approach: "If I don't do chores, I get punished by not being able to go to a friend's house."

■ **Earning more.** Some Just-Because kids get their allowance money and that's it. They can't earn more from their parents. But about half the kids on this plan sometimes earn more by doing extra chores at home. They have an Extra-Chores Option added to their basic allowance plan. So do most Chores Plan kids, as you'll see in the next section.

Extra-Chores Option

This option makes dirt look mighty attractive—the dirt messing up grimy cars or grungy basements, to name two filthy possibilities. Cleaning away the dirt can fatten your wallet if you install an Extra-Chores Option in your allowance plan. That's what most members of our Allowance Squad have done. They often pocket more than their usual allowance by taking on out-of-the-ordinary chores. Kyle does extra chores just about every week. David does them a few times a month. "Sometimes my parents ask me to do something extra. Sometimes I ask them," says David.

What qualifies as an "extra"? That depends on a kid's regular duties. Jennifer says an extra is "something my mom doesn't feel like doing." This All Star sometimes cashes in by vacuuming, not her regular job. Matt's regular chores include things like table setting and garbage lugging. For him, mowing the family lawn is a good summertime extra. Snoop around. You may uncover lots of extras that parents would gladly pay you to do.

How to arrange a fee for an extra? David's parents set his, which is fine with him since the fees are usually fair. If an offer seems low, some kids do a bit of careful negotiating to get it raised.

Payday Possibilities

■ **How often.** Most Squad members receive their allowance every week. Some get it less often—every two weeks or once a month. Stephen likes getting paid each week. "Once a month is too long to wait. Sometimes I need money at short notice," he says. Katie explains, "We decided on a weekly allowance because it's an easy time period for me to budget." But Charles likes getting his allowance once a month. "That lets me plan better what to do with it," he says. "If I got it once a week, I might waste it on little things. By getting it once a month, I get more money at one time and can save it up to buy better stuff."

■ **Hand-It-Over System.** This is pretty simple: Allowance payday rolls around, and a parent hands over the cash. Most kids on our All-Star roster get paid that way. No problem—unless the parent forgets or doesn't have the right change. (More about that later.)

■ **No-Hands System.** A few kids don't get their hands on their cash at all on payday. Parents hold the allowance for them or deposit it into the kid's bank account. The kids (or a parent) keep a record, adding in each payday's new amount so they'll know how much the kids have stored up. Some kids keep these records in a book. Lizzie's dad uses a computer. "I just use a plain sheet of paper," says Ms. Buie, a financial planner who uses this system with her daughter.

What if kids want cash to buy something? If their money is in the bank, they go and take some out. If parents hold the cash, kids simply ask for what is needed (in person or with a note). Nicole writes checks ("play" ones) to give her parents, who then hand over the amount on the check. After that, records are updated to subtract what the kids got.

Complicated? You bet! It's only for families who will stay on top of all that record keeping. Some kids like this system. It helps them *think* before blowing a wad since they have to go through such a big deal to get their cash. Nicole notes that "my parents usually give me the money when I write a check, if it's not for something stupid." She uses a kit made for this kind of system. The kit comes with play checks and a checkbook in which to record how much she gets and spends. "It helps me keep track of my money," she says.

Other Choices

■ **Fouling out.** Some Chores Plan kids lose dough if they don't finish their chores, but do they lose out for other kinds of

misbehavior? Some do—being naughty may get them "docked" (part of their allowance is held back). But most kids say that never happens. Their parents use other ways to handle misbehaving.

■ **Kits.** Several ready-made allowance kits are available, besides the one Nicole uses. (See page 28) But kits have a big drawback: The plan a kit uses may not fit the goals you and your family have worked out for your allowance. Some kits use chores setups. Others, like Nicole's, use a checkbook system. Kits are also costly, ranging from $15 to $40. (See page 83.)

However, you can easily make your own homemade "kit,"

using supplies you already have at home or that you buy at a stationery or office-supply store. You'll probably spend less and get *exactly* what you need for your own special allowance plan, whether it's a big wall calendar to keep track of paydays, poster board for making a chores chart, a spiral notebook for record keeping, notecards to use as "play" checks, or a little booklet of receipts (which would also work great as "play" checks). "It doesn't have to be a fancy system," says Ms. Buie. She and her daughter do just fine with their own homegrown sheet-of-paper system for keeping track of allowance money.

> *"If I don't do chores, I get punished by not being able to go to a friend's house."*

The Write Step

After you and your family figure out your allowance plan and all your extra options, it's smart to write the plan up so everyone is clear about what's expected. "We sign a contract, just like real life," says Stephen's mom.

But *wait!* Before signing anything, there's another biggie to work out—MONEY! For a look at the money picture, move on to the next page.

The Money Picture

What a Difference!

Some kids on our Allowance Squad get as little as fifty cents a week in allowance. A few (a *very* few) claim to rake in a whopping $20 or *more* in allowance a week. YIKES! But most have a more medium-sized allowance—from $1 to $5 a week.

Age has a lot to do with these differences. Older kids tend to get bigger allowances than younger ones. For example, Sarah gets more at age eleven than when her allowance started, back when she was six. Other things also affect allowance rates, such as what families can afford or what expenses the allowance is to cover. Kids who have to use their allowance to pay for basics like school supplies, school lunch, or clothes may pocket a larger allowance than those who use it just for fun extras.

If the allowance is tied to chores, the number of chores can also affect the rate. More duties may mean more dough. "When we got a dog, I had to feed and pick up after her so I started getting more allowance," says Matt.

"We decided how much allowance I'd get based on the amount of work I do."

There's More!

Is the cash Jennifer gets for allowance her only income? No way! Like many of our All Stars, she also earns money by working for neighbors. "I baby-sit or take care of people's pets," she says. She also picks up a little spare change doing extra chores at home and sometimes cashes in at birthday or holiday time by receiving gifts of money from relatives.

Several research studies have shown that most allowance kids are like Jennifer—allowance isn't the only way they get money. Some actually earn more from odd jobs and extra chores than from allowance. So is the allowance still important? Absolutely! As Jennifer explains: "You can't always get jobs like baby-sitting, but the allowance is always there."

Rates Roundup

Several groups have done big surveys to find out typical allowance rates. The following charts show what two surveys found.

What Zillions Found . . .

	AGES 9 AND 10	AGES 11 AND 12	AGES 13 AND 14
ALLOWANCE	$3 a week	$5 a week	$5 a week
TOTAL INCOME (Allowance plus extras)	$7 a week	$13 a week	$20 a week

SOURCE: *Zillions*, April/May 1995.

This chart shows allowance rates reported in 1995 in *Zillions* magazine (the kids' version of *Consumer Reports*). The magazine surveyed 800 kids and found the "median" amount that the kids with allowances got. Median means half the kids got that much or less—half got that or more. The magazine listed rates for allowance *and* total income (allowance plus cash from jobs, extra chores, gifts, etc.).

What Nickelodeon Found . . .

	AGES 6–8	AGES 9–11	AGES 12–13	AGES 14–15
ALLOWANCE	$2.57 a week	$4.62 a week	$6.85 a week	$9.36 a week

SOURCE: The Nickelodeon/Yankelovich Youth Monitor ™, 1997.

This chart shows average allowance rates from a 1997 survey of 1,600 kids done by the Yankelovich Partners research group with the TV network Nickelodeon. These rates are a bit higher than those reported by *Zillions*. That may be because of how the results were calculated, using the "average" (or "mean"), which tends to be higher than the "median."

Picking Yours

Surveys like those you just read about give an idea of what some kids earn. You could do your own mini survey, asking friends what they get. But their rates may not end up being the same as yours. As Stephen's mom notes, "Every family has a different situation."

To pick *your* rate, you and your parents need to sort out:

- What things you're supposed to pay for with your allowance and how much they cost.
- How much your parents can afford to give you.
- How much cash you feel you can really handle.

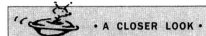

• A CLOSER LOOK •

Bobby's Mini Survey

Before setting his allowance rate, Bobby and his mom first talked with other families in their neighborhood about how much their kids got for allowance. "We found that parents that had more money were giving more," Bobby says. "But my family is so big we couldn't afford that much." He and his mom agreed on an amount they both could live with. "It's okay," he says. "I can earn more doing extra chores."

An allowance needs to be big enough so you have some cash to manage and save. But don't make it so big that it would be a major disaster if you fumble now and then and blow it all on some spur-of-the-moment silliness. (After all, nobody's perfect—goof-ups *do* happen.) Other tips to keep in mind:

"Some of my allowance has to go in the bank for college."

- **Bargain.** Katie asked for one amount. Her parents offered half as much. They settled on a rate midway between the two.
- **Work it out.** If you have a chores allowance, figure out how much each job is worth. "We decided how much allowance I'd get

based on the amount of work I do," Larry explains. Julia's mom's rule: "The harder the work, the more the pay."

• **Go easy.** Be sure parents are really cool about the rate so the allowance doesn't flop later when they realize they can't swing it.

Money Rules

Some families set rules about what kids can do with their allowance money; other families don't. Our All Stars do well both with rules and without them. It depends on a kid's personality and the family's style. Independent-minded go-getters may soar with no rules, while other kids may feel more comfortable with a few guidelines.

Kelly explains her family's rules for her allowance: "Once a month I have to make a deposit in my savings account. I can't spend allowance money on junk, only on stuff that's worthwhile." Having to make those deposits helped Kelly save for a video game. Andy's allowance has a college clause: "Some of my allowance has to go in the bank for college." Other families have rules about setting aside some allowance money for charities, to get kids in the helping habit.

Money rules earn a thumbs-up from Ms. Buie. As a financial planner, she gets lots of calls for help from adults who are absolutely terrible at managing money. She thinks money rules may help kids learn how *not* to end up that way as adults. She has these rules for her own daughter's allowance:

- $1 is for anything her daughter wants;
- $2 has to be saved for gifts;
- $2 has to be saved for something special that will take her daughter a while to save up for.

Other kids don't have to follow any special rules on how they can spend their allowance. Their families prefer letting the kids figure things out on their own. "I can spend my allowance any way I want," says Stephen. How has he done? Super! He has even invested some of his money in the stock market. Katie, another no-rules kid, made some buying goofs at first, but says,

"Now I'm more careful." Matt also doesn't have any rules to follow. But before buying something big, "my parents ask why I want it," Matt notes. "I usually only buy stuff I need."

> *"I can't spend allowance money on junk, only on stuff that's worthwhile."*

Advances

"If I need a little extra money, I ask my mom if she'll pay my *next* week's allowance in advance," says Larry. "I still do my chores the next week. I just don't get paid that week." Lauren can get advances, too. "Only for special things," she notes. But if Nicole goes broke, she has to wait until her next payday to get her allowance. "My parents said no advances," Nicole explains.

Before trying to talk your folks into giving an advance, be warned that many parents have strong feelings about this. Some parents feel if kids keep getting extra cash whenever they run out, the kids will never learn to manage money. But other parents believe an advance—for a *moderate*

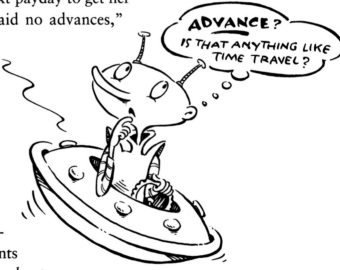

amount—may help kids learn some useful lessons, too. If you get less than usual one payday because you've already gotten some allowance money early, you'll have to figure out a way to make do with less. Maybe you'll even decide to start saving up an emergency fund for unexpected expenses. As Ms. Buie, the financial planner, says: "If it's a reasonable advance, okay. But if parents let it slide and don't care how many months in advance kids get allowance, that's a bad lesson."

Another warning: When people get a loan from a bank, they have to promise to pay back both the amount they borrowed plus a little more (called "interest"). An allowance advance is sort of like a loan. Some parents may suggest charging you interest on it. However, none of the parents interviewed for this book do that.

If you end up like Nicole and can't get an advance, try her back-up strategy. Whenever she *really* needs extra cash for something, she uses the Extra-Chores Option (see page 25). Slogging away at extra chores has a special bonus: It gives you time to *think* about what you're dying to buy. Is it really worth it? Or will it just gather dust (along with all those old games you never touch anymore)? Smart questions to ask before any purchase.

QUICK CHANGE
A survey of sixth, seventh, and eighth graders around the country found that most would be willing to give some of their allowance money to a charity to help feed hungry children in poor countries.

SOURCE: Childreach, *1992*.

How to Get Paid on Time

> MY DAD CAN REMEMBER BATTING AVERAGES FROM 25 YEARS AGO! SO WHY CAN'T HE REMEMBER TO PAY MY ALLOWANCE ON TIME?

Busy, Busy, Busy

Parents' less than perfect memories earn a lot of grumbles from our team of Allowance All Stars. Most gripe that their parents sometimes forget to hand over allowance cash on time.

But, hey, parents aren't the only forgetful folks. Kids sometimes forget to *ask* for their money. If you have soccer practice, scouts, music lessons, a spelling test, and a big project to worry about, no wonder allowance day might slip your mind.

Parents forget for the same reason: They have so much to do! Most pay up when they finally remember. But one girl says, "If I don't remember to ask for it, I don't get it." Another girl notes that forgetfulness isn't always the cause of a pay delay. "Sometimes my parents have a lot of bills to take care of," she says. "I understand and don't say much." But if the culprit is just plain old ordinary forgetfulness, here are some ways to make remembering allowance day easier for parents—and kids, too.

Move It

Maybe the day your family set as allowance day is too crammed with activities and errands for an overworked parent to remember your cash. If so, move your payday to a less busy day of the week or to a day parents *always* link with money—*their* payday. "I get paid every two weeks when my parents get paid," says Matt. Charles moved to a monthly payout when the payday at his mom's job switched to once a month. A monthly allowance payday has a big advantage for forgetful moms and dads—fewer allowance paydays for them to remember.

Mark It

"I mark my allowance days on the calendar," says Stephen. A big family calendar in a busy spot like the kitchen is a great way to keep track of paydays as well as all those activities that keep everybody on-the-go. Leaf through the calendar and mark each of your allowance paydays in a colorful, hard-to-miss way.

A calendar can also help end those frustrating did-you-get-paid arguments. Jesse writes a note on the calendar when he gets his allowance. If there is no note on the calendar one week, that proves he didn't get his cash that week. One mom jots a note on the calendar if she doesn't have the right change to pay allowance one week as a reminder to pay up later. Some kids use chores charts as payday reminders. To get his cash, Derek shows his parents his chart with the chores nicely checked off.

Don't Get It

Another way out of the forgotten-allowance trap: Don't get paid—in *cash*, that is. If you're good at record keeping, consider a No-Hands System. Parents hold your allowance for you or deposit it into your bank account until you need it. You keep a record of how much they (or the bank) are keeping for you. As long as you always use dates when each new amount is added to your record, you can tell in a flash if a week's payment got skipped. If so, you can easily add it in. (See page 27.)

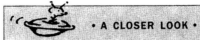

• A CLOSER LOOK •

Katie's Exact Change

Getting paid the right allowance right on time—that's something Katie can usually count on, thanks to her mom's special Friday routine. Katie's mom has gotten into the habit of walking out of her office each Friday after work and heading straight to the bank across the street. "I get enough cash out of the bank for Katie and her sister so I can pay them the right amount when I get home," explains Katie's mom. "I do weekly budgeting and am getting money out for other things at the same time. So it's not hard to remember."

Check It

Emily's mom never forgets to have enough cash on hand for allowance day. She pays Emily by *check*. "When my mom does the bills on the computer at the end of the month, she also prints out a check for me," says Emily. "It encourages me to save rather than spend." To turn that check into money, Emily has to cash it at a bank. "I usually just put it in my bank account," she says. If she wants to buy something, she can either take money out of her account or use extra cash she has earned by baby-sitting.

Do It

A hot tip from the mom of an Allowance Squad member: "When I have to *nag* a lot to get chores done, I don't feel like paying up." If you do your fair share (without *too* much moaning and groaning), you might notice a remarkable improvement in your parent's on-time pay-out record.

Hint, Hint

Last but not least, try Michael's strategy: "Remind, remind, remind." But watch out! "Don't get parents ticked off by whining. Parents don't want to be nagged," says Dr. Eugene Beresin, a psychiatrist who admits to having been late in paying allowance sometimes himself. "Give them a helpful reminder, just as you would want them to give you a helpful reminder if you forgot to brush your teeth. Don't harass them or make them feel like they're failing. If their intentions are good but they can't keep it together, organize it for them. Write out what they owe you, like a little accountant. If you seem organized and responsible, most parents will be wowed by that."

Here are our All Stars' oh-so-careful ways of reminding:

- "I write a note on a sticky pad and put it on the refrigerator." —Ryan
- "My mom has a beeper. I leave messages on it about my allowance."—Latisha
- "I remind them how good the yard work I did looks."—Randy
- "I remind my mom on the phone before she comes home from work."—Christy
- "I remind my dad on the day *before,* to make sure he has the right change for my allowance the next day."—Jill (Some parents keep a stash of singles in a secret spot and restock it once a month so they'll always have the right change for *all* the next month's allowance paydays.)
- "If my dad doesn't have the right change, I write out an IOU." —Lauren

Memory Saver

If *you* are the forgetful one who can't remember to ask for your allowance, maybe money isn't so important to you yet. That's okay. When you need it, you'll start remembering. But if all that forgetting bugs you, set a goal of something to save up to buy. That might help you remember to ask for your dough.

Trying for a Raise

Game Plan

Magic might not get you a raise, but a careful game plan may do the trick. Half of our Allowance All Stars asked for an allowance raise in the year before filling out questionnaires for this book. Most of those brave raise seekers hit the jackpot and ended up with a bigger, juicier allowance. Maybe not as big and juicy as they wanted, but more than they used to get. The winning play that led to success? "Explain *why* you deserve the raise," says Mike. Also helpful: a cool, calm presentation. Here's how those raise winners did it, plus tips from some moms and dads on what does (and doesn't) work with parents.

Scouting Reports

The first step for several of the kids who got raises was to hunt around for facts to back up their case. That's actually what career counselors recommend that grown-ups do before asking for a raise at work. Grown-ups are often advised to write a report that shows how important they are to their company and how they're being underpaid. Most kids didn't actually write a report. But in talking with their parents, the kids made good use of the facts they'd gathered. (However, a short write-up might be smart—to show how mature you are.)

Here are the kinds of facts kids uncovered:

■ **On pitching in.** "I listed all the chores I did so my mom would realize how much I *really* did," explains Amanda B. Jill listed the many chores she did, plus the many *fewer* ones her younger brother did. She told her dad, "I do a lot more than my brother, but you give me only a dollar more. Tell me if I'm wrong, but that's not quite fair." Her dad gave her a raise. Stephen's mom suggests another way Chores Plan kids might talk parents into a raise—by showing that "an allowance chore is more difficult or takes longer to do than originally anticipated."

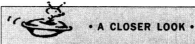

• A CLOSER LOOK •

Julia Takes Charge

"When I asked for a raise, I told my mother that now that I'm a junior high-er, there's more money involved," says Julia. "I talked with her one afternoon when she was in a good mood. I said I needed to buy more stuff than when I was younger. If I didn't have more allowance, I'd be left out of a lot of after-school activities. I said I'd take over some expenses my parents would have paid for, like school dances and other activities." Julia likes the raise she got—and the challenge of paying her own way more.

■ **On expenses.** Mike got his raise by listing the kinds of things he usually buys to show that his allowance wasn't quite large enough. Julia pointed out that her expenses went up when she started junior high. Good strategy, says Emily's mom, who recommends showing real "examples of how expenses have increased." For instance, parents may not realize how much more a pack of sports cards costs now than a few years ago. Bring your folks up to date.

- **On money savvy.** "I told my parents I deserved more money because I knew how to spend and save," says Sam. It might help to keep a list for a few weeks of what you do with your cash to show just how money wise you are. Point out if you've saved up to buy something special—or if you're saving up for something now. That can show parents that extra cash given to you won't be wasted. (By the way, this would *not* be a good time to blow your whole allowance on sugary sweets.)

"I told my parents I'd do more chores."

- **On rates.** David found what other kids earned in order to point out that his allowance was kind of low. If you poll your friends, ask them what they have to pay for with their allowance—your parents may want to know. Lizzie supported her claim of being underpaid by "showing my dad a copy of *Zillions* magazine with allowance rates." However, these strategies might not work with some parents, like the mom who claims, "I don't *care* what other families pay!" A dad advises using the friends-get-more argument *only* if you can prove it. Michael says he used a different kind of fact about rates—that his hadn't gone up in a few years. "I explained that I thought I was old enough for more money," he says. He got his raise.

Bargaining Chips

Many kids offer to *do* something in exchange for a raise. "I told my parents I'd do more chores," says Larry. Great idea, according to several Allowance Squad parents. Julia offered to pay for more things. Her raise wouldn't increase her parents' expenses since she'd pay for things they used to pay for. A dad suggested linking the increase to a certain kind of purchase, such as getting a separate clothing allowance. You could also try a bargaining trick that has often helped adults in wage negotiations: Ask for a slightly *bigger* raise than you want so you can give in a little and still come out okay.

Pre-Game Warm-Up

■ **In the mood.** To get parents in a generous mood before a raise request, Brendon says, "Do lots of stuff to help out and be nice to your brother or sister (if you have one)." This tip earns applause from our parent advisers. Lauren's mom says she'd be more likely to give a raise if the child "does chores without being asked or nagged." Julia's mom adds, "A job well done is noticed. Thrill me and deserve a reward."

"If you want more allowance or any new privilege, such as staying up later, think about the things that win parents over. One is school. School is your 'work,'" says Dr. Beresin. "Try to get good grades. Another is keeping up with your responsibilities at home, like making your bed. And try not to fight too much with your brother or sister.

The more mature parents think you are, the more things they'll let you control on your own"—money or other freedoms.

As you plan your mood-setting good deeds, it might be wise to spend several days (or even—*gasp!*—a few weeks) on them rather than a rushed pre-request half hour of top behavior (which might actually turn parents *off* rather than on).

■ **Run-through.** "I planned what to say in advance," says Amanda B. "That way it sounds more convincing." Some kids find it hard to talk about money. So do grown-ups! If you've got the jitters, calm down by rehearsing your request. Try it out on the bathroom mirror, the nearest tree, or your favorite pet.

Show Time

"I had my raise talk with my parents at night because during the day they're so busy and have other things on their minds," says Amanda B. Find a quiet time to talk when parents can stop rushing around and really listen to your request. It might help to set up the talk in advance, rather than springing it on them. Some kids talk with both parents, but Larry pitched his request just to his mom. "She's the one who takes care of the allowance," he says.

"Act mature," suggests Heather. Keep cool and calm, especially if parents make a few requests, too. When Andy asked for a raise, his parents agreed *if* he'd promise to put more money in his bank account. No sweat. What if parents criticize how you do your chores? Try a tactic adults use when negotiating with a boss at work: Ask for a list of goals on how to improve your performance. Set up a trial period (in which you'll try to meet the goals) and a follow-up meeting for discussing the raise again. What if the talk gets hot and you start to lose your cool? Call it quits and try later when all's calm.

Back-Up Positions

Some Squad members asked for a raise and struck out. You may, too, on your first try. Maybe money is tight in your family. Wait until things ease up before popping the question again. Or maybe your presentation isn't convincing enough. If so, work on it. Gather more facts, think up more offers, keep up with your responsibilities—and consider two other options:

■ **Bonus.** Companies often use a bonus to reward workers instead of giving a raise. It's cheaper to pay a one-time bonus than to shell out more money every week in a raise. Is there a mega extra chore at home you could do for a major bonus?

■ **Odd jobs.** Neighborhood jobs boost many kids' incomes. Heather mows neighbors' lawns, Derek baby-sits, Desirée waters plants, Randy shovels snow and cleans garages. For job ideas, ask friends or go to the library for books on kids' jobs or on making things you could sell. (See page 82.)

No-Hassle Raise

Kyle doesn't go through a big deal to get a raise. His raises are automatic. "I get a fifty-cent raise every year on my birthday," he says. An automatic yearly raise can save a heap of trouble. You and your parents could agree to have a raise review each year at a certain time—your birthday or the start of the school year. Some families raise the allowance by the same amount each year. Others base the raise on a kid's responsibilities and expenses that year.

Raise No-No's

Here's what *won't* work in getting a raise (according to Allowance Squad parents):

- Whining
- Begging
- Asking for way too much
- Making a lot of foolish purchases
- Not doing chores on time
- Running out of money often
- Saying, "*Everyone* gets more!" (unless you have proof)

Don't Blow Your Dough

Join the Crowd

Kid *gets* allowance—kid *blows* allowance!

It happens, even to kids on our Allowance Squad. "When I first started getting an allowance, I spent it all on candy," says Sarah. "There were two problems with this. I got sick, and I had no money left for other things I wanted." Sarah wised up. So did most of her Squad mates. She stopped snapping up every gooey goodie that caught her eye. "I learned to save my money until I know what I *really* want," she says.

Blowing a few bucks on candy isn't so bad if that mistake changes you into a champion saver. But it's not always easy to turn off the money faucet—especially with all the pressure on kids to buy, buy, buy. Companies spend millions on ads aimed at kids, ads that make you laugh and give you cool jingles to sing, all the while tempting you to spend your cash on their products. If you keep ending up broke buying things you wish you hadn't, you may need help to tame the spending habit. Check out these tricks Squad members use to get their cash under control.

Which Way Did It Go?

The first step in curbing runaway spending is to figure out where your money goes. "I thought of a way to keep track of it," reports Jill. "I keep a chart in a notebook." On the chart, she writes how much money she has, when and why she got it, as well as when and why she spends it. "Now I know where my money goes," she says. "If I'm saving for something, I put a note along the side of the chart, like: 'Don't spend. Save for Father's Day gift.'" This money diary has helped Jill a lot, although she says, "Sometimes it's a pain to record everything."

Using a money diary for just a week can pay off, too, as Miranda discovered. She wondered why she couldn't save up for things. She found out after keeping a money diary for a week. At the end of the week she added up all the little purchases she made and was shocked to see she'd spent about the same amount she took in all week long. "I never knew I spent *so much* in one week," she says. She decided to make some changes: "I wish I hadn't spent so much on ice cream. I want to open a bank account so I can be more careful."

Spread It

Another cash-control tip: Stuffing your *whole* allowance in your pocket (or wallet) makes it way too easy to get at—and spend on tempting spur-of-the-moment junk. Instead, many kids stash their allowance in a few different spots. "I have two little banks in my room," says Amanda B. "One bank is in the shape of a dog. I put part of my allowance in it for long-term saving (like when I saved up for a lamp). The other bank is a cow. I put the rest of my allowance in there for everyday spending. If I'm saving for something, I put more than half in the dog bank. If

I'm not saving for anything, I put more in the cow. If I go some-where, I take a little out of the cow to put in my wallet."

That pooch and cow also help her not *lose* her cash. "Once I stuck my allowance in my closet and couldn't find it later," she says. "Now I put it in my dog and cow banks right away."

Adrian splits her allowance in half. Each week she puts half in a savings account until she needs it for something special. She keeps the other half at home for spending money. Other kids have *several* money spots, using envelopes, bottles, boxes, or jars. They mark each one for a goal (such as holiday gifts, music, snacks, charity) and divide their cash among the containers. If they want a new rock album, they use only cash in the music jar. Some kids use locked containers to keep out their greedy fingers—and those of pesky brothers or sisters, or even a dad looking for change for the pizza person. To make a multi-container system work smoothly, it helps to get paid allowance in small bills or coins so it's easier to divide up.

QUICK CHANGE
About 66 per cent of kids between the ages of twelve and fifteen have a savings account.

SOURCE: Teenage Research Unlimited, 1996.

Plan It

It also helps to think about exactly how you want to divide up your dough. Some kids simply work out a plan in their heads for what to do with their allowance. They don't actually write anything down. But other kids write down a plan. You can, too, by mapping out information like this:

- **What I Have:** How much money you take in each week, plus how much you've got saved up.
- **What I Want:** What you want to buy right away, as well as what you want to save up to get later.
- **What I'll Do Each Week:** How much of your cash you'll set aside each week for each thing you want.

The official name for a plan like this is the dreaded "b" word: "Budget"! That word scares lots of kids—and grown-ups, too! It sounds so formal and complicated. But it's not that hard. Maybe if you don't call it a "budget," it might not seem so tough. Call it anything you like—a map, a guide, Uncle Aldo, or whatever. But the few minutes you spend planning this watcha-ma-call-it will help *you* stay the boss of your money.

"I always write up a budget for holiday gifts and special big things I want," says Amanda H. "For holiday gifts, I write up a list of all the people I need to buy gifts for. Then I figure out how much money I'll have for all the gifts and divide it evenly among them." Next, she thinks up gifts to get each person and heads to the store. "If I go over the limit for one gift, I spend less than I planned for another so it evens out."

Grow It

A super spot to park cash so it's way out of reach is a savings account. "I keep money in the bank so I can't spend it fast even if I wanted to," says Imogen. Trudging to a bank to get cash gives you plenty of time to think before you blow it. Besides, the longer you park your money in the bank, the richer you'll get—thanks to good ol' *interest*. That's money a bank pays you for lending it your cash

• A CLOSER LOOK •

Michael's Gamble

"Mom takes some money from my allowance and holds it until I have $50," says Michael. Then she writes a check so the $50 can be deposited in an account Michael has at a "stock mutual fund."

A mutual fund puts together money from Michael and its other members to buy shares of stock in many companies. Those stocks make fund members part owners of the companies. If the companies do well, the value of the stocks may go up and Michael's account will earn money. But if the stocks go down, his account will *lose* money.

It's a gamble. Unlike banks, stock investments aren't insured. But he's gambling with only *part* of his money. He has some tucked safely in a bank.

"My aunt knows about stocks and helped me pick a good fund," he says. He opened the fund account with her since kids can't buy stocks on their own. To learn more, talk with your parents and check out library books on investing. (See page 82.)

for a while. It's not a fortune, but every bit helps.

Noah had about $375 in his savings account and earned nearly $10 in interest all year. The interest is added in gradually over the year so the *interest* earns interest, too! Be sure to use a bank that will pay interest no matter how little is in your account. Some banks charge fees if an account has less than $500, but many won't do that on a kid's account. Another plus: Banks are insured. Even if a bank goes out of business, you'll get your cash.

Adrian goes to her bank every Saturday to add cash to her account. Katie makes deposits once a month, using her "personal banker" (her mom). "I give money to my mom and she makes the deposits," says Katie. Other kids are less regular. "I make a deposit when I have more than $50 at home," says Randy. If it's hard finding time to bank, do it by mail: Give cash to a parent, who'll write a check you can mail in with a deposit slip.

Extra Growth

If you don't plan to use your savings for a few years, consider:

■ **U.S. Savings Bonds.** They pay more interest than savings accounts, can be bought at a bank for as little as $25, but can be cashed in only after you've had them for six months.

■ Certificate of Deposit (CD).

At most banks, you need $500 or more for a CD account, which usually pays more interest than a savings account. But to get *all* the interest, you have to leave your cash in the account for a set period, such as a year.

Go for the Goal

It can be hard to make yourself save if you don't have a good reason to do it. Think of something you'd like to save up for—something so terrific you'd even pass up buying candy for it. Start small, with a goal that can be reached in only a few weeks. Scoring big on that first goal will prove that you really can save. Then, shoot higher and save up for something bigger.

"I keep money in the bank so I can't spend it fast even if I wanted to."

"Put a picture of what you're saving for in your wallet or on your piggy bank so you remember to save and not spend," says Emily. Michael notes, "If you're tempted to buy something, think how far it will put you from what you *really* want. The sooner you save, the less chance it will be sold out or gone."

Touch Control

What about kids who might dip into their "Saving-for-a-Mountain-Bike" jar in order to scrape together enough coins to see the latest hit movie (for the *fourth* time)? Randy's advice: "Let your parents hold the money you want to save." Or try a No-Hands System. (See page 27.)

More Money Tips

- "I keep my allowance under control by making sure I don't spend more than half of it at one time."—Maggie
- "If I have $10, I'll spend only $5 max. To spend $10, I wait until I save $15."—Kyle
- "Before I buy anything, I ask myself: 'Do I really want this? Do I need it? Or am I buying just to buy?' Then I sleep on it before I decide to buy."—Jill
- "Once I took all my money to a store and spent it. Later I wanted to buy something else but couldn't. I learned never to take *all* my money to one store, just the amount I'll need."—Charles
- "I shop around for the best buy."—Jill

- "When I bought a stereo, I checked a few stores to see where it was cheapest."—Larry
- "Stuff that costs less is often the same as stuff that costs more."—Kyle
- "If it's an expensive item, Matt pays part (usually half) and we help out with the rest."—Matt's mom
- "I try to go 'looking' (not 'shopping') at different stores *without* spending. Then I'll go back to the store I found most interesting."—Kelsey

Buying Report

What do the 166 kids on our Allowance Squad buy with their allowance?

- **Fun.** Most spend some of their allowance on fun things, such as tapes, games, toys, and hobby supplies.
- **Snacks.** About one-third of them munch away at least part of their allowance.
- **Clothes, gifts.** Less than half buy clothes or gifts.

Only a few use any of their allowance for necessities like school supplies or school lunch. Surveys by Nickelodeon and *Zillions* also found that kids spend their money mainly on fun extras.

Fixing Fizzled Allowances

Fix-it Tips

About one out of every four kids on our Allowance Squad spent some time at the Fix-it Bench, looking for ways to rescue allowances that have temporarily crashed.

They discovered an important tool in repairing a broken allowance—having the guts to speak up! Bobby *wished* he'd done that at the first sign of allowance trouble. Instead, he went on strike. "I stopped doing my chores because I was sick of them," he says. The result? His parents stopped paying him. After many weeks of this, he began to hurt—in his wallet. "I wanted to go out with my friends, but I didn't have any money," he recalls. So Bobby and his folks finally had a talk. It took a while to sort things out, but they found a way to get his allowance going again. "Instead of just stopping the allowance, I should have talked with my parents about the problem sooner," Bobby says.

"I should have told my mom about my problem with my chores *before* she got mad," says Kathleen. When her mom threatened to ground Kathleen if she didn't start doing her allowance chores, Kathleen realized she better do some talking—fast. "Don't wait," advises Kathleen. "If kids have problems with their allowance, they should see their parents immediately."

Chores Changes

Undone chores were the main cause of allowance breakdown for Kathleen, Bobby, and other Squad members as well. Kathleen's repair trick: Trade in chores you hate for ones you'd like better. While talking with her mom, Kathleen said she didn't do her chores—washing sinks—because she didn't like doing that. "Mom said it was okay if I changed the chores I didn't like with my sister, who doesn't mind doing sinks," notes Kathleen. "So now I do the dusting and windows. My allowance is going great now."

Bobby had to do some serious negotiating to persuade his parents to give him a second chance. "They were angry about me not doing my chores," he says. "So I added in a few extras, like taking out the garbage and sweeping." He also gained a fresh outlook on chores after talking with his parents. "We talked about responsibility and how my mom had a hard time doing everything herself," says Bobby. "I'm more willing to do chores now because I see my mom and dad really need my help."

Chores Cheers

Some All Stars prevent allowance breakdown by finding ways to make allowance chores less of a pain:

- "I listen to music. You pay more attention to the music than to not wanting to do the chores."—Amanda B.
- "I listen to TV while doing my chores."—Katie
- "I do the hardest one first. That makes the rest seem easier. Or I try to make a game of it. I pretend I'm playing football when I run from one chore to the next."—Mike
- "Get your chores over with and think of the fun things you'll do after they're done."—Heather.
- "I time myself to see how fast I can do them."—Manda
- "I do the part of a job I don't like first to get it over with. I don't like unloading the bottom rack of the dishwasher. I do that first. I save the top rack with the cups for last. I like that best."—Sarah
- "Think of the money you'll get."—Heather

Memory Boosters

■ **For kids.** Some allowances break down because kids keep forgetting to do their chores. To give their memories a boost, many All Stars put up a chores chart. Others get into a groove and do a chore at the same time each day (or week). Charles's strategy: "Each day I make a list of everything I have to do." Sarah gets some back-up help: "If I forget, my parents remind me."

■ **For parents.** When Kathleen and her mom had their fix-it-up chat, Kathleen explained *another* reason she stopped doing her chores: She was ticked off that her parents sometimes forgot to pay her allowance on time. Their solution: "After I do a chore, I tell my mom right away and she pays me right then," says Kathleen. (For more memory joggers, see pages 42–47).

Switching Plans

Sometimes just swapping chores or posting a chores chart may not be enough. A major change might be needed—switching to a different allowance plan. (Turn back to pages 18–30 for lots of plans and options that might rescue a sinking allowance.)

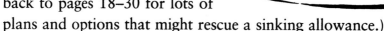

Divorce Dilemma

Some Squad members say their allowance stopped when their parents got divorced. It's understandable that an allowance might break down temporarily when such a big change occurs. But once a new routine gets worked out, kids can try to get the allowance going again. Kids should ask their divorced parents to talk with each other about the allowance so they can agree on how it will work. Both parents need to agree on which parent will give the allowance, how much it will be, and what the rules will be.

Asking Grandpa

"I was in sixth grade when my allowance began. It was twenty-five cents a week." Eric was amazed when his grandpa told him that. Only a *quarter!* Of course, it was 1920. Things were a bit cheaper then. A fistful of candy cost just a penny!

Asking parents or grandparents what they got and spent as kids might be a good way to get an allowance talk going. (Grown-ups *love* to talk about the "old days.") That might help you in pointing out to them how much *higher* the cost of kid-living is now. They may remember money tricks that helped them stop blowing their cash as kids—ones that may help you, too. Or if your allowance is on the fritz, maybe together you can think up ways to fix it.

If those things don't get worked out, problems can pop up. For example, one parent might try to win a kid's favor by handing out a lot of extra money, much more than the other parent can afford. "At first it seems like a great deal," says Dr. Beresin, a psychiatrist who has worked with kids in divorced families. "Eventually that will backfire. As children get older, they'll realize they were being bought off. They'll see that what counts is how much the parent really cares about them."

Kids can help by giving divorced parents a nudge in the right direction. "Say to the parents, 'Please work it out with each other.

Don't use us as Ping-Pong balls,'" advises Dr. Florence Kaslow, another therapist who helps families deal with divorce. "Money shouldn't be used as a bribe."

Waiting Game

■ **Wrong time.** One Squad member says his allowance started too soon. He was so young he wasn't interested in money yet. He'd forget to ask for it—his parents forgot to pay it. So they waited a few years until he woke up to the wonders of money.

■ **Tight times.** "My allowance stopped for a while when my dad lost his job and *he* needed the money," says one Squad member.

> ### QUICK CHANGE
>
> A *Zillions* magazine survey found that kids who didn't have an allowance got about the same total weekly income as allowance kids. But no-allowance kids felt less good about what they got and how they handled it.
>
> SOURCE: *Zillions*, April/May 1995.

"If a parent can't afford to give an allowance, I've found that kids can be very understanding," says Dr. Beresin. "It hurts, especially when other kids have money to spend and you don't. But there are other treats a parent can give that don't cost money—such as doing interesting things together—so you won't feel so deprived." Waiting paid off for that Squad member. When things eased up financially for his family, his allowance started again.

Keep At It

Is a fizzled allowance worth fixing? You bet. You'll get a steady supply of cash *(yes!)*, plus a chance to learn how to be money smart. That will come in handy as you move into the world of big bucks and big bills a few years down the road. "My allowance helped me learn not to waste my money so when I'm older I'll know how to use money," says Nikki. Jennifer agrees: "I've learned when to keep it, save it, or just have fun with it."

Troubleshooting Guide

To help keep your allowance rolling along, check out the handy guide that starts on the next page. It shows where to look in this book to see how other kids have dealt with some common allowance problems and gripes. But first, here's a helpful hint for *any* allowance problem: A friendly brainstorming session with Mom or Dad can work wonders in helping you find good ways to fix an allowance gripe. As Kathleen says (on page 69): "If kids have problems with their allowance, they should see their parents immediately."

Allowance Problem or Gripe	What to Do About It	See page(s):
If you're unhappy with how much money you get for allowance . . .	• Try for a raise (*after* you first plan a raise-asking strategy).	48–55
	• Do extra chores at home for extra pay.	15, 25–26, 40, 51, 54
	• Earn money doing odd jobs in the neighborhood or selling stuff you make.	32, 55, 82
	• Hang on to the money you already have so it lasts longer.	56–67
	• See how your allowance compares to others.	33–34, 50, 51
If your parent keeps forgetting to pay allowance on time . . .	• Change your payday.	42–43
	• Switch to a No-Hands System or an automatic-deposit plan.	27–28, 44
	• Get paid by check.	44–45
	• Use a calendar or other memory joggers.	43–47
If you keep blowing your allowance on little junky stuff and can't seem to save . . .	• Keep a money diary.	58–59
	• Stash cash out of reach.	59–66
	• Set a savings goal and make a spending and savings plan.	61–62, 65–66
	• Get your allowance less often.	26–27
	• Have your parent (or a bank) hold your money for you.	27–28, 44, 62–65
	• Get paid by check.	44–45
	• Have a parent set spending rules for you.	37–39
	• Go "looking" instead of "shopping," and use other tricks for hanging on to your cash.	66–67

Allowance Problem or Gripe	What to Do About It	See page(s):
If you hate the chores you have to do for your allowance (or keep forgetting to do them) . . .	• Try to change your chores.	19–20, 22–24, 70
	• Find ways to make those chores less dreary.	20, 22–23, 71
	• Use chores memory joggers.	20–22, 72
	• Consider using a different allowance plan.	18–30, 72
If you keep losing your allowance . . .	• Find some safe places to stash it—and put it there!	59–60, 62–65
	• Switch to a No-Hands System or an automatic-deposit plan.	27–28, 44
	• Get paid by check.	44–45
If you've got *almost* enough allowance saved up for a special event this week, but need just a *little* bit more . . .	• Ask for an advance.	39
	• Do extra chores at home for extra pay—or a job for a neighbor.	15, 25–26, 32, 40, 51, 54–55, 82
If your allowance has crashed . . .	• Try to figure out what went wrong and talk things over with your parent.	68–75
	• Brainstorm with your parent about different ways to set up the allowance.	18–30
If you're having trouble persuading your parent to start an allowance . . .	• Explain how an allowance can help you become money wise.	6–8
	• Show how an allowance can be convenient for parents, too.	9–10

Resource List

Suggestions for further reading and additional information, plus how to contact some of the organizations mentioned in this book.

Books

If your allowance isn't big enough to cover all your money needs (and you've already tried asking for a raise), check out your local library or bookstore for books on how to earn extra cash. Two good books to look for:

Better Than a Lemonade Stand by Daryl Bernstein (Beyond Words Publishing, 1992).

Making Cents: Every Kid's Guide to Money by Elizabeth Wilkinson (Little, Brown, 1989).

You might also look for books on how to make your cash grow, such as:

Banking by Nancy Dunnan (Silver Burdett Press, 1990).

The Stock Market by Nancy Dunnan (Silver Burdett Press, 1990).

Kits and Catalogs

Although you can easily round up all the allowance-running supplies you'll need at a stationery or office-supply store (see page 29), several ready-made allowance kits are available. However, a ready-made kit may not really fit your needs since it may set up an allowance differently than you'd like. But if you're kit-curious, you could contact:

ParentBanc
1920 Nacogdoches, Suite 101
San Antonio, TX 78209
800-471-3000

This is the checkbook kit Nicole used. (See page 28.)

National Center for Financial Education
P.O. Box 34070
San Diego, CA 92163-4070
619-232-8811
Website: www.ncfe.org

This organization puts out a catalog that offers several chores-based kits as well as quite a few books on money management for kids and parents, too.

About the Allowance Squad

All-Star Roster

Out of a pool of about 280 students in eleven schools around the country who filled out four-page questionnaires on their spending money, 166 made the final cut and became part of the Allowance All-Star Squad. Why did those nine- to fourteen-year-olds make the team? Because they were the ones who got an allowance! But a big cheer of thanks goes to all the kids—allowance getters or not—who filled out those long questionnaires (and to the dozen parents of Squad members who filled out special parents' questionnaires).

Coaches

Thanks also go to the following educators who arranged for students to fill out questionnaires for this book: Bonnie Barry, State College Junior High School, State College, Pennsylvania; Maureen Cardozo, East Middle

School, Modesto, California; Jeff Cohen, P.S. 29, Brooklyn, New York; Pat French, Saints Simon & Jude School, Louisville, Kentucky; Herb Hinz, Ebeling-Utica Schools, Mt. Clemens, Michigan; Susan Mallett, Thomas L. Head Elementary School, Montgomery, Alabama; Caroline McDowell, Hamblen Elementary School, Spokane, Washington; Marian Pedersen-Grover, Fishkill Elementary School, Fishkill, New York; Sharon Vardian, North Royalton Middle School, North Royalton, Ohio; JoAnn Weatherbee, Rockland Middle School, Rockland, Maine; Ross Wersonick, Mohave Valley Junior High School, Mohave Valley, Arizona.

Squad Boosters

Special thanks go to the following advisers who were so helpful in sharing their views on kids and money: Dr. Eugene Beresin, Harvard Medical School; Dr. Jonathan Bloomberg, Rockford (Illinois) Memorial Hospital; Elissa Buie, certified financial planner, Institute of Certified Financial Planners; Dr. Ken Doyle, University of Minnesota; Tom Drew; Gloria Goldstein; Dr. Florence Kaslow; Dr. Lawrence Kutner, *Parents* magazine; Professor Jeylan T. Mortimer, University of Minnesota; Phyllis Stein, Career Programs, Radcliffe College; Professor Viviana A. Zelizer, Princeton University. Information from the April/May 1995 issue of *Zillions*, published by Consumers Union of U.S., Inc., Yonkers, New York, a nonprofit organization, is printed by permission. Thanks also go to two other Allowance Squad fans—Ellen Clyne and Soyung Pak.

978-0-595-39106-6
0-595-39106-0

CPSIA information can be obtained at www.ICGtesting.com
Printed in the USA
LVOW131008220212

269858LV00003B/83/A